AF413098

An Indigo Blue Adventure
HAPPY KINDNESS DAY
Haven 101 Press ~ Rockville
BY TOM DOYLE
ART BY POLINA POVSHEDNA

*Be kind to love.
Love to be kind.*

Thanks to LVW—This book would not happen without you.

Today is a wonderful day,

it is Show and Tell Day.

What shall I share?

A leaf, a book, or

my prize from the fair?

TOYS

As I skip to school,

I think of something very cool.

What I can share with my class

is even better than

my purple giraffe!

Today, I will share

how I have created a day,

a day that we all

can live in a special way.

Today, I will share

Happy Kindness Day.

HAPPY KINDNESS DAY

Happy Kindness Day is for us all,

to remember to do something nice,

no matter how big or how small

Perhaps the gift of a smile

to another who has been

sad for a while . . .

. . . Or a hug

for a special someone

to remind them

they are number one.

DKS

Happy Kindness Day

is a reminder to everyone,

that small acts of love

can always be done.

Happy Kindness Day reminds us

to think of something nice to say

to make others feel great

in their own special way.

you have the prettiest eyes!
you are amazing!

It does not take much

to do a kind deed,

like teaching another

to learn how to read.

We let others know

by our acts and our deeds

that kindness can spread love,

like planting small seeds.

JOY
LOVE
PEACE

So, I will show and tell

my friends

that Happy Kindness Day

never ends.

Every day

is the perfect day

to say

"I want to make this

a Happy Kindness Day."

OCTOBER
1 2 3 4 5
6 7 8 9 10 11 12
13 14 15 16 17 18 19
20 21 22 23 24 25 26
27 28 29 30 31
happy :)

My name is Indigo Blue,

and this is what I like to do.

In your own way,

every once in a while,

how can YOU

make someone smile?

Indigo Blue Adventures

Happy to Be Me

Happy Kindness Day

Indigo Blue and Demontreus Too!

Visit us!

Website: IndigoBlueAdventures.com

Instagram: @indigoblueadventures

Meet the Creators of *Indigo Blue Adventures*

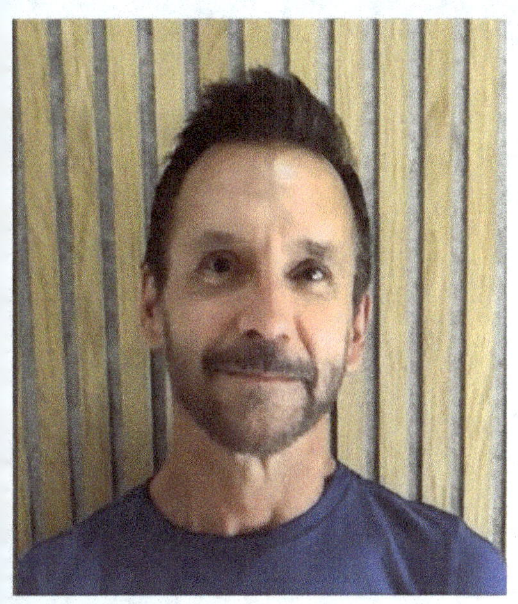

Tom Doyle, a native of the Washington DC area, is not only an accomplished trial lawyer but also a passionate author of children's books. Inspired by his experiences reading with his own children, he strives to empower young minds to embrace their uniqueness and become the best versions of themselves. Beyond his professional life, Tom finds fulfillment in his spiritual journey and serving the world around him. He is the creator of EquanimiChi, a breath to movement system, and also offers various other healing practices at Haven 101, the Wellness Center he founded.

Polina Povshedna is a children's illustrator from Odesa, Ukraine. She believes that youth literature serves as a great opportunity to stop, relax, and spend quality time with children, learn something with them and discuss their emotions. Polina and her own children read books before bed every evening and it is her favorite part of the day. She loves seeing the world through children's eyes and creating something for children that will evoke their emotions. Her dream is to write and illustrate her own book and dedicate it to her children.